Languages of the World

French

Anita Ganeri

www.raintreepublishers.co.uk
Visit our website to find out
more information about
Raintree books.

To order:

☎ Phone 0845 6044371

🖷 Fax +44 (0) 1865 312263

🖳 Email myorders@raintreepublishers.co.uk

Customers from outside the UK please telephone +44 1865 312262

Edited by Dan Nunn, Rebecca Rissman, and Catherine Veitch
Designed by Marcus Bell
Picture research by Ruth Blair
Originated by Capstone Global Library
Printed and bound in China by South China Printing
  Company Ltd

ISBN 978 1 4062 2448 1 (hardback)
15 14 13 12 11
10 9 8 7 6 5 4 3 2 1

ISBN 978 1 4062 2455 9 (paperback)
18 17 16 15
10 9 8 7 6 5 4 3 2

British Library Cataloguing in Publication Data
Ganeri, Anita
French. -- (Languages of the world)
440-dc22
A full catalogue record for this book is available from the
British Library.

Acknowledgements
We would like to thank the following for permission to
reproduce photographs: Alamy pp. 5 (© Danita Delimont),
7 (© Penny Tweedie), 8 (© Ancient Art & Architecture
Collection Ltd), 21 (© Ken Gillespie Photography), 25
(© Tim Kavanagh / Conceptual); Corbis pp. 13 (© Anna Peisl),
15 (© Hugh Whitaker/cultura), 16 (© Birgid Allig), 20
(© Frank Schnabel), 22 (© Charles Platiau/Reuters);
Shutterstock pp. 6 (© Dmitriy Shironosov), 9 (© J.M.P.M.
Seijger), 10 (© Andresr), 11 (© Valentyn Volkov), 11
(© ntstudio), 12 (© Ekaterina Pokrovsky), 14 (© Monkey
Business Images), 17 (© Monkey Business Images), 18
(© Muriel Pichon), 19 (© Fotomicar), 23 (© Monkey Business
Images), 24 (© jackhollingsworthcom, LLC), 26 (© Isabella
Pfenninger), 27 (© Nikolay Stefanov Dimitrov), 28
(© ESLINE), 29 (© fcarucci).

Cover photograph of a boy reproduced with permission of
Corbis (© Paule Seux/Hemis).

We would like to thank Severine Ribierre for her invaluable
help in the preparation of this book.

Contents

French words are in italics, *like this*. You can find out how to say them by looking in the pronunciation guide.

French around the world

French is the main language of France. It is spoken in more than 50 countries around the world. It is also spoken in some parts of Canada, Belgium, Switzerland, and Luxembourg.

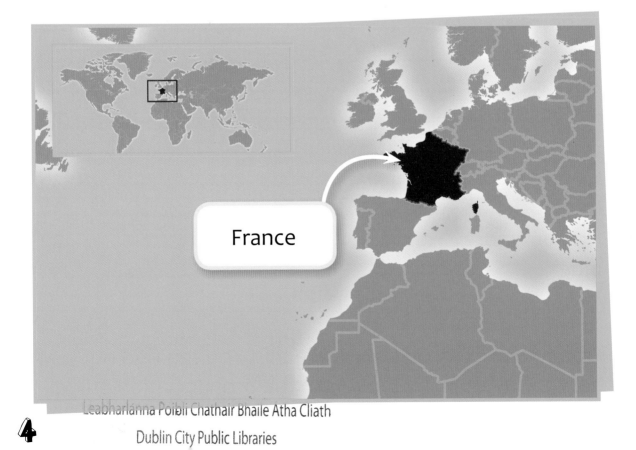

France

"Manquez pas le bateau"

CENTRE CHOUIN' ART
Le pêcheur

OUVERT DE

Restaurant
Poissonnerie
Dégustation

fumé & mariné

How to say it
France = *la France*
French (language) = *le français*

Millions of people in Africa also speak French. They live in countries that France once ruled. In French, the countries where French is spoken are called *la Francophonie*.

Who speaks French?

About 140 million people speak French as their first, main language. About 190 million more speak French as their second language.

Chatting to friends is a good way to practise speaking French.

Many people speak French in Africa.

French may sound very different when it is spoken outside France. People say words in a different way. They also use words borrowed from other languages.

French and English

French is called a "Romance" language. This is because it comes from Latin. Latin was the language spoken by the Romans. English does not come from Latin. English is not a Romance language.

Some old buildings have Latin writing.

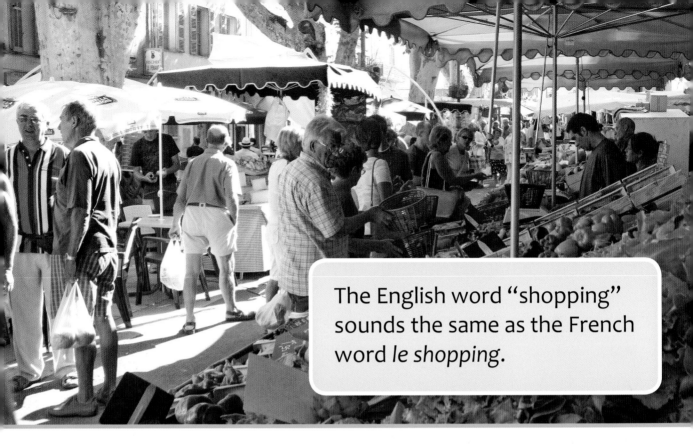

The English word "shopping" sounds the same as the French word *le shopping*.

Some French words are used in English, such as *café* and *ballet*. Some English words are used in French, such as *le shopping* and *le week-end*. Can you guess what the words in the box below mean?

la banane　　*le chocolat*　　*la famille*　　*la plante*
(See page 32 for answers.)

Learning French

French uses the same alphabet as English but some letters are said differently. The best way to learn French is to listen to how French people speak and try to copy them.

How to say it
yes = *oui*
no = *non*
thank you = *merci*

Words that name things are called nouns. In French, nouns are feminine or masculine. If a noun is feminine, the word for "the" is *la*. If a noun is masculine, the word for "the" is *le*.

Saying hello and goodbye

Friends and family usually kiss each other several times on the cheek when they meet. They may say "*Salut!*" People say "*Bonjour!*" or "*Bonsoir!*" to be more polite.

How to say it
Hello (to friends) = *Salut!*
Good day/morning = *Bonjour!*
Good evening = *Bonsoir!*

Salut can mean "goodbye" as well as "hello". There are different ways of saying "See you again". People say "*Au revoir!*" or "*A bientôt!*" *Bonne nuit* means "goodnight".

Talking about yourself

To tell someone your name you say
"Je m'appelle ... " ("My name is ...").
To tell them how old you are, you say
"J'ai [huit] ans" ("I am [eight] years old").

How to say it
My name is ... = *Je m'appelle ...*
I am ... years old = *J'ai ... ans*

To tell someone where you come from you say "*Je viens de ...*" ("I come from ..."). If they ask you if you speak French you can say, "*Oui, je parle français!*" ("Yes, I speak French!").

15

Asking about others

To ask someone what their name is you say "*Comment tu t'appelles?*" "*Quel âge as-tu?*" means "How old are you?"

How to say it
What is your name? = *Comment tu t'appelles?*
How old are you? = *Quel âge as-tu?*

How to say it

Where do you live? = *Où habites-tu?*
  or *Où habitez-vous?* (polite)
Do you speak English? = *Parles-tu*
  anglais? or *Parlez-vous anglais?*

To find out where someone lives you can ask "*Où habites-tu?*" To ask if they speak English you can ask "*Parles-tu anglais?*" If you are talking to someone older use *vous* instead of *tu* to be polite.

At home

Homes in countries where people speak French can be very different. In cities people often live in apartments or flats. Some apartment buildings are new, but many are very old.

How to say it
house = *la maison*
flat = *l'appartement*

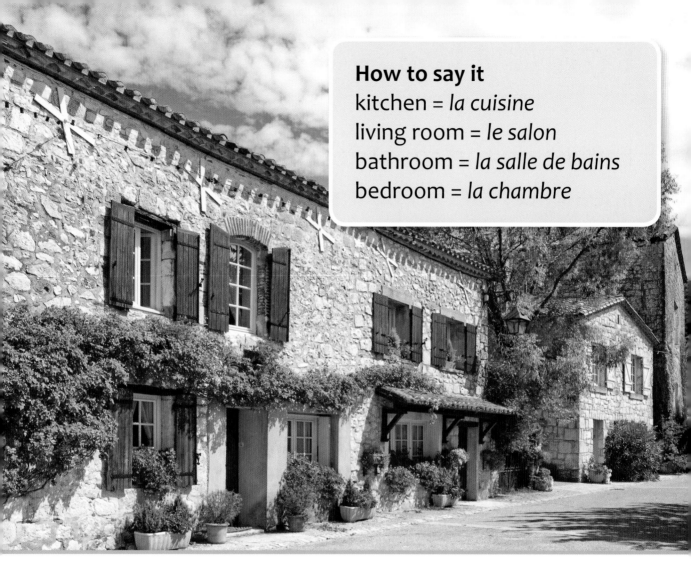

How to say it
kitchen = *la cuisine*
living room = *le salon*
bathroom = *la salle de bains*
bedroom = *la chambre*

In the countryside people usually live
in houses. Some are large and old, like
this one. Others are modern. Some large
country houses are called *châteaux,*
which means "castles".

Family life

Families in the countries where people speak French can be large or small. In some places, children, parents, and grandparents all live together in the same home.

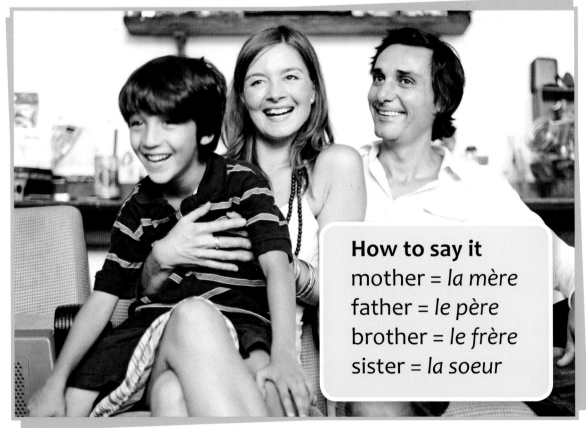

How to say it
mother = *la mère*
father = *le père*
brother = *le frère*
sister = *la soeur*

The French word for "family" is *la famille*. This family is out for a winter walk in Canada. They are taking their dogs with them. The French word for "dogs" is *les chiens*.

At school

In France children go to primary school from the ages of 6 to 11. Then they go to a middle school until they are 15 years old. They go to high school from age 15 to 18.

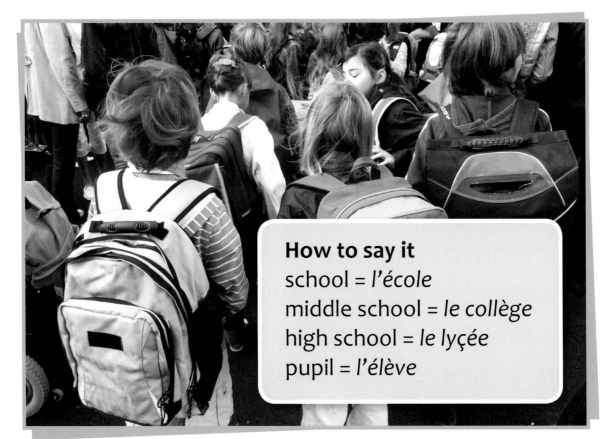

How to say it
school = *l'école*
middle school = *le collège*
high school = *le lyçée*
pupil = *l'élève*

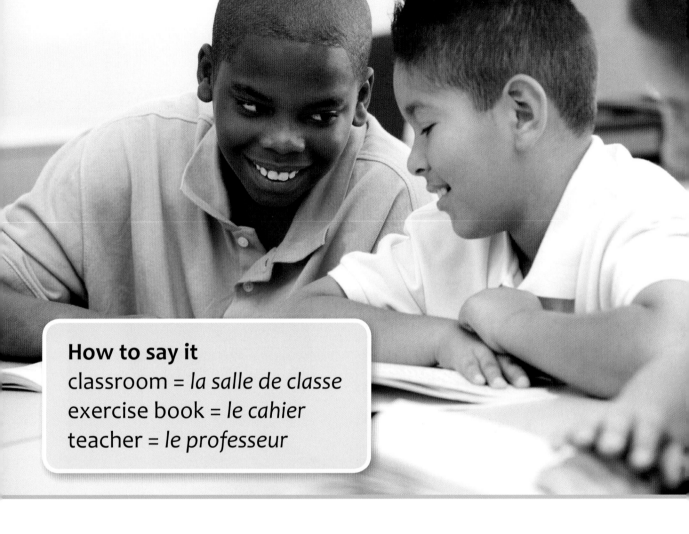

How to say it
classroom = *la salle de classe*
exercise book = *le cahier*
teacher = *le professeur*

At school children learn many different subjects, including French. Children in countries that do not speak French may also learn French at school.

Having fun

People in French-speaking countries like doing many different things in their spare time. They listen to music, go to the cinema, and enjoy going to cafés.

How to say it
music = *la musique*
cinema = *le cinéma*
café = *le café*

In many French-speaking countries football is popular. People in France also like cycling, tennis, and playing *pétanque*, which is a type of bowls.

Food

French food is famous all over the world. In France, people like to eat long loaves of bread called *baguettes*. These are freshly baked every morning.

How to say it
bread = *le pain*
fruit = *les fruits*
vegetables = *les légumes*

How to say it
cheese = *le fromage*
paté = *le pâté*
I'm hungry = *J'ai faim*
Enjoy your meal! = *Bon appétit!*

Lots of different kinds of cheese are eaten in France. The French word for "cheese" is *le fromage*. *Paté*, which is made from meat, is also popular.

Clothes

What clothes do you like wearing? Most people who live in French-speaking countries probably wear the same sort of clothes as you! In French the word for "clothes" is *les vêtements.*

How to say it
clothes = *les vêtements*
jeans = *le jean*
T-shirt = *le tee-shirt*
jumper = *le pull-over*

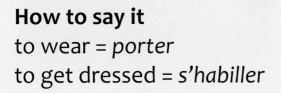

How to say it
to wear = *porter*
to get dressed = *s'habiller*

In some French-speaking countries in Africa people wear brightly coloured robes. You may see African people in France wearing these clothes, too.

Pronunciation guide

English	French	Pronunciation
apartment (flat)	*l'appartement*	*lapartemon*
aunt	*la tante*	*la taant*
bathroom	*la salle de bains*	*la sal de ban*
bedroom	*la chambre*	*la shambr*
bread	*le pain*	*le pan*
brother	*le frère*	*le frair*
café	*le café*	*le cafay*
cheese	*le fromage*	*le fromaaj*
cinema	*le cinéma*	*le seenayma*
classroom	*la salle de classe*	*la sal de klass*
clothes	*les vêtements*	*lay vaytmon*
Do you speak English?	*Parles-tu anglais?*	*Paarl too onglay?*
Enjoy your meal!	*Bon appétit!*	*Bon appaytee*
exercise book	*le cahier*	*le kayay*
father	*le père*	*le pair*
football	*le football*	*le footbal*
fruit	*les fruits*	*lay frwee*
get dressed (to)	*s'habiller*	*sabeeyay*
goodbye	*au revoir!*	*oh revwar*
good day/morning	*bonjour!*	*bonjoor*
good evening	*bonsoir!*	*bonswoir*
goodnight	*bonne nuit!*	*bon nwee*
grandfather	*le grand-père*	*le gronpair*
grandmother	*la grand-mère*	*la gronmair*
hello	*salut!*	*saloo*
high school	*le lycée*	*le leesay*

house	*la maison*	*la mayzon*
How old are you?	*Quel âge as-tu?*	*Kel aaj a too?*
I am ... years old	*J'ai ... ans*	*Jay ... on*
I come from ...	*Je viens de ...*	*Je veean de ...*
I'm hungry	*J'ai faim*	*Jay fan*
I speak ...	*Je parle...*	*Je paarl*
jeans	*le jean*	*le jeen*
jumper	*le pull-over*	*le pewl-over*
kitchen	*la cuisine*	*la kweezeen*
mother	*la mère*	*la mair*
music	*la musique*	*la mewzeek*
My name is ...	*Je m'appelle...*	*Je mappel*
no	*non*	*non*
paté	*le pâté*	*le patay*
pupil	*l'élève*	*laylev*
school	*l'école*	*laykol*
See you soon	*A bientôt!*	*A beeyanto*
sister	*la soeur*	*la sir*
sitting room	*le salon*	*le sallon*
sport	*le sport*	*le spor*
teacher	*le professeur*	*le profaysir*
tennis	*le tennis*	*le tayniece*
thank you	*merci*	*mairsee*
the	*le (m); la (f)*	*le; la*
T-shirt	*le tee-shirt*	*le teeshirt*
uncle	*l'oncle*	*lonkl*
vegetables	*les légumes*	*lay laygewm*
wear (to)	*porter*	*portay*
What is your name?	*Comment tu t'appelles?*	*Common too tappel?*
Where do you live?	*Où habites-tu?*	*Oo abeet too?*
yes	*oui*	*wee*

Find out more

Books

50 French Phrases, Susan Martineau (b small publishing, 2009)
First French Words, Neil Morris (Oxford University Press, 2007)
French is Fun with Serge, the Cheeky Monkey!, Sue Finnie
(dvd activity pack: BBC Active, 2006)

Websites

kids.nationalgeographic.com/kids/places/find/france
www.bbc.co.uk/schools/primaryfrench/

Index

Meaning of the words on page 8

la banane = banana
le chocolat = chocolate

la famille = family
la plante = plant
